WHY YOU NEED JESUS

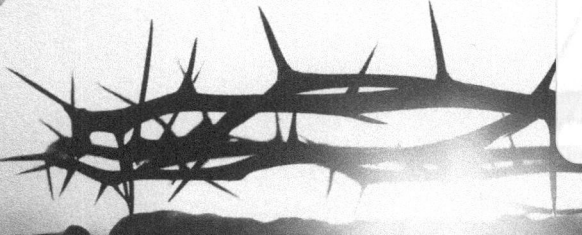

JESUS CHRIST IS LORD

JAMES STAMPS

WHY YOU NEED

JESUS

JESUS CHRIST IS LORD

JAMES A STAMPS

Kravitz & Sons
INNOVATORS IN PUBLISHING, MARKETING AND ADVERTISING

Kravitz and Sons LLC
204 E Arlington Blvd. Suite B
Greenville, NC 27858

Published by Kravitz and Sons LLC.

ISBN: 979-8-89639-343-6 (sc)
ISBN: 979-8-89639-345-0 (e)

Library of Congress Control Number: 2025916428

Table Of Contents

DEDICATION

I dedicate this book to our Lord and Savior Christ Jesus.

I also want to dedicate this book to my wife who has gone on before me to be with the Lord and Savior Jesus and am pleased to know that she is with him in Heaven, a much better place to be than here on the earth. Of course, while here on the earth we want to do all that we can for the Lord and with every effort seek to please him in all that we do.

ACKNOWLEDGMENT

Having been taught in this world to make a mark of worthiness for yourself to others I have sometimes tried to move and maintain in such a way that shows me as a helper, or servant to others; in fact, I have seen it written in various places that the name James means "helper", or one who comes to serve and not to be served. In writing the contents of this book I am doing so to share some of the experiences that I have had in walking with Christ Jesus. You must develop a relationship with Christ Jesus to avoid the "magnets" pull of the world on you to make a lot of wrong decisions with your life activities. Jesus will always guide you in the right direction for your life when you yield it to him. I thank all of my friends and family who have been an inspiration to me in writing this book to reach people and tell them how Jesus has helped me to know how valuable and wonderful it is to accept him as Lord and Savior early in my life.

ABOUT THE AUTHOR

I was born in the State of Arkansas, United States of America. Our family lived in a house that was quite a way back into the woods; the best part of being in the woods was the tall pine trees plentiful and readily available for the purpose of cooking, heating the rooms and using the fireplace. While growing up I watched my dad cutting down the trees for the firewood, and anxious to do the same thing myself not knowing that the day would be coming soon when I would have to be the one gathering the wood. It was a real pleasure knowing that we had our own home because that was quite an unusual thing to see for most people to own a home in those "lean" years.

Very early in life I became interested in school and asked my mother if I could go to see the school that I would be attending when I become 6 years of age. The problem with that timing was that I was only 5 years old but wanted to see what it was like before I had to go; in other words, one might say do a reconnaissance and be prepared. She let me go to check it out and as soon as I arrived at the building and started up the stairs leading to the entrance door, I was hindered by a guy standing there, which called me a name that I didn't like. I decided that the sensible thing to do was to ignore this person, so I turned and went back home.

It was a long walk through the woods to get to the school building, but at the age of 6 years, I enjoyed it and even ran a lot of times. Best of all it was time to be there, and I gained a lot of respect. I found the school attendance to be enjoying learning new things every day.

The other good thing about our school was that it was right across the road from a church, so I felt good about the school's location. The somewhat funny thing about this school was that it was equipped with a large cast iron stove to provide heat for the people, and whenever we had a recess, we would run out the door to play games, but as soon as we were starting to play the teacher would begin tapping on the window saying "Boys, Boys, go into the woods and gather some wood for the stove. Well, you can imagine how we felt about that chore, nevertheless, we did it quickly.

I was really happy when I completed school there and entered High School in a different location and didn't have to go through the woods anymore. I always considered anything that I accomplished with excellence that it was Jesus, the one to get the praise.

As you read this writing you may see that I was not a professional writer but one who looked to the Lord to help me complete the task.

INTRODUCTION

The purpose of this writing is to introduce you to our Lord and Savior Jesus and to show you, the reader, what is the most important thing that you can and should do immediately if you have not already, and that is to ask and receive Jesus our Lord and Savior into your heart for Salvation of your Soul.

Jesus Christ Is Lord

Some of us distinguish him as Christ, the anointed one, and his anointing given to him by God, who is our Father, who makes us joint heirs with his son who gave his life and shed his blood on the cross at Calvary, which is the required sacrifice for the forgiveness of sin.

"Wherefore God also hath highly exalted him and given him a name which is above every name: That at the name of Jesus every knee should bow, of things in heaven, and things in earth, and things under the earth; And that every tongue should confess that Jesus Christ is Lord, to the glory of GOD the Father."

(Philippians 2:9-11)

All of this is such an easy thing to do, yet most do not want to do it. I pray that all come to know the truth and receive Jesus as their Lord and Savior now. Many people think he was just a good man during his appearance here on earth, but it is far more than that.

"Jesus saith unto him, I am the way, the truth, and the Life: no man cometh unto the Father, but by me. If ye had known me, ye should have known my Father also: and from henceforth ye know him and have seen him."

(John 14:6-7)

With that being said, we ought to pay heed to what he has said more earnestly and do it. With all of the previous explanations,

I will start here to provide my testimony as to why I feel so strongly about accepting Jesus as the only way to the Father, as he said, *"No man cometh to the Father but by me."*

I also believe that being raised in a family that had received Jesus, had a lot to do with one being protected even before personally receiving the Lord and Savior Jesus as I know I was.

Starting with a time in my childhood when having a meal at the table, had to quote a scripture given to us even if we didn't know the why of it; perhaps not the best way to start, but at least a good start to what would be better later.

My verse was,

> *"I AM the True vine, and my Father is the Husbandman."*
> ### (John 15:1)

And now, for the start of my learning of things on the earth. When I was about three years of age (not having understood the concept of aging), one day, I entered the dining room of our house and smelled my mom baking cookies. She had just completed the task and came into the dining room and was holding a plate well loaded with cookies right in front of me, close enough that I could have taken one off the plate. I was standing there near the table, thinking I would get to eat several of them, but that wasn't the case, as she said we would have to wait until morning to have them.

Being the obedient person that I was to my mom, I agreed to my mother's orders. I must have been awake all night, wishing and anticipating the morning's arrival. As soon as it was daylight, I got up and headed to the dining room. Earlier, I had watched her placing the plate containing the cookies on the very top shelf of the China cabinet in the corner of the dining room.

Remember now, she had promised that I could have some of those cookies in the morning, and it was morning, so I decided to get the plate. As little as I was, I had to move a chair from the dining table, place it against the China cabinet, and climb onto the flat section of that cabinet so that I could stand and reach the plate of cookies resting on the top shelf inside the glass door enclosure. This cabinet had two sections to it. The lower section was wider than the upper section, providing ample space to stand on or place things on it.

The first thing I noticed was that the door was already open, but why was it open; who had beat me on the cookies? I knew I could not remove the plate itself, so I stretched to a point where I could reach far enough to grab a couple of cookies off the plate. Having noticed that the glass door was partially open, it was not enough to comfortably reach inside to get to the plate of cookies even though it had been closed the day before. I opened it a bit further and reached for the cookies on the plate. Much to my surprise, as my hand should have touched the cookies, I felt something that moved slightly at a slow pace; and I didn't feel anything like the cookies I had seen on that plate.

My first thought was that because Mom had so many cookies piled on the plate, perhaps, she had placed something around the edge of the plate to hold the cookies on so they wouldn't slide off.

I proceeded to reach farther because I had seen the cookies on that plate, but I was not tall enough to see the plate on that top shelf. I decided to stretch and reach even further. I made contact with the unknown object, and it moved again. This meant that two long-shaped things had moved.

Well, I had gone this far, so I decided to try once more; I did and felt the same object move, only this time, all three of the log-shaped things snapped vigorously into a 'braced' or very tense position. My reflexes took over me, and I jerked my hand back. I did not do this out of fear because I had no fear of anything, nor had I been taught about fear.

One might question that if I had no fear, why did I remove my hand so quickly? Well, simply because of the built-in reflexes, one action gets a reaction. Now I am asking myself what could be on that plate that moved and left no cookies that I could feel; so, I climbed back down to the floor, turned and faced the kitchen door, and called out very loud for my dad, not having any idea where he was, nor even if he was up from the bed yet. Instantly, he came rushing in from outside to see me and had an annoyed look on his face that said, "What now?" as I had never had to raise my voice that loud for anything.

He said nothing. As soon as I saw him, I didn't say anything either, but without ever looking toward the China cabinet, I merely pointed stiff-armed towards the top shelf where the door stood open. I was very angry because I found no cookies after waiting all night to get them. He casually walked over there and was tall enough to see what I had not seen but had felt with my right hand. With one quick look, he turned and ran with a speed that I believe would have set an international speed record going back through the door to the kitchen and through the outside door of the house.

Now, I was left wondering what to do as running was not an option for me because I had just had my hand on all three rolls of the plates occupant and was not hurt. A minute or two passed before he returned carrying a pitchfork, proceeded to the cabinet, and impaled it with brute force. For those who don't know what a pitchfork is, it is a large metal fork with a long wooden handle commonly used to bail (lift) hay on the farm.

Next, he pulled the fork out with the plates occupant wrapped around it and slammed it against the wall by the baseboard and onto the floor. I could see my dad's teeth, as he appeared to be smiling and having fun, making me think this must be one of our pets that I hadn't seen. After all, we did have cats and dogs. Remember now that I had never been taught about dangers on the earth, nor learned about these critters, so there was no fear instilled in me, which leads me to now believe that the display of his teeth was a sign of aggression and his anger at the fact that it was now being eliminated after it has invaded our privacy.

After wrestling with this "thing" for a while, the action stopped. Dad left the room carrying it on the pitchfork and never spoke to me from the beginning to the end. I wish he would have told me what that was because, as life goes on, things happen as they did what I believe was the very next day. As I was sitting there on our back porch, an identical creature of the same type in the house passed by me, heading west as the sun rose in the east, giving a bright glow to the copper color on its head.

I noticed it crawling by slowly, so I decided to catch it to show my dad it was just like the one he had taken out of the China cabinet the day before. Because the sun was striking its head, it highlighted the vivid copper color. After many attempts hurrying to close my hand onto it to pick it up, my hand wouldn't close, no matter how hard I tried. It soon reached a point where it crawled under a log we had lying there on the edge of the yard. I later learned that this is a type of poisonous viper, a Copperhead moccasin, as they are a viper related to the Cobra family.

Praise the Lord Jesus for his divine protection.

"How shall we escape; If we neglect so great salvation; which at first began to be spoken by the Lord, and was confirmed unto us by them that heard him; God also bearing them witness, both with signs and wonders, and with divers' miracles, and gifts of the Holy Ghost, according to his own will?"

(Hebrews 2:3-4)

One day, a few years later, I got the chance to receive Jesus for myself. It took place at our church. We were approaching the end of a revival service for the week. At the end of the service, I jumped up and proceeded to the altar with the altar call request to receive Jesus into my heart.

On the way, some people told me that I was too young to know what I was doing and should wait until I was older. However, nothing could stop me as I wanted this more than anything I could think of. I believe if l had not received Jesus, I would not be here right now with all of the close encounters with disaster. It was like the enemy had come to kill, steal and destroy me.

"These things I have spoken unto you, that in me yet might have peace. In the world, you shall have tribulation: but be of good cheer; I have overcome the world."

(John 16:33)

See why you need Jesus?

Next, I was Baptized in a creek of running water and rose to the feeling that the *kingdom of heaven* had opened right in front of me; it was a glorious and memorable experience that I love, even now. To everyone on earth, you should receive Jesus into your heart as soon as possible, *"Now is the appointed time,"* because I believe this is the greatest action you can experience here on earth.

I must warn you an enemy is still accessing this earth and is not your 'friend.' He comes immediately to take away what you have received and continues to try even if he fails initially. Keep your heart well attended, remembering that the battle is the Lord's, so don't try to fight it on your own.

Moving on, I had a lot of other close calls with disasters, but I won't go into all those at this time. The next one was when I was about 11 years old when some neighbors moved in close to where my aunt and I lived.

She had asked me to stay with her to assist her with the chores. I want to mention that as young as I was then, I helped family members and friends build that house. I still remember the times I smashed my thumb while hammering in nails and exclaiming, "Ouch! that hurt," but I continued with the task.

The neighbors also built a house a short distance from us and had two boys about my age. We soon started to travel around the area together, going to church, hunting, harvesting their crops, and riding bicycles.

One night, as we were walking home from what I believe was a church service, we were very close to the point where we would turn off the gravel road and proceed up the hill on a sandy road to the house when we could hear the sound of hammering in the woods emanating from the opposite direction of where we would be going. We got curious and decided to check it out.

As we approached the sound's origin, we saw flames and heard voices. When we were very close, the noise stopped. We stood there a few seconds before, and suddenly, guns started firing toward us. We ran and managed to run fast enough to avoid being hit, or it seemed that way.

We split up as we ran. I took a short path toward the house, which happened to cross a cactus field that no one I knew had ever traveled across, as there was no good way of crossing the cactus. I will always believe that I was carried across that field by the Lord our God because I didn't feel my feet touch the ground until I felt the ground on the other side of it.

Later, we found out that it was a distillery making moonshine. With that, our investigation of the noises came to an end.

Praise be to our Lord and Savior Jesus for taking care of us.

The house I was born in had a piano in the living room and an organ in the hallway. I spent a lot of my time playing both, hoping one day to play the instrument in church or on a stage.

One day, our dad was working in the field southwest of the house while My mother and I were home. Naturally, I played the piano on the southwest side of the house while she prepared lunch. After a little while, I heard her say, "Stop playing. I hear someone yelling loudly."

As soon as I stopped playing, I heard my dad calling to us about a fire to get out or something similar. Within a few seconds, he was at the back door telling us to get out as the whole south side of the roof was on fire!

Had he not been there to warn us, the whole south side roof would have fallen on us. I believe it would've been lethal and would've killed us!

You see, we had those 'shake shingles on the roof, which were very dry. I'm sure the heat from the wood stove perhaps generated sparks and the sun were the cause of the fire. By this time, the neighbors about a mile away had noticed the flames and rushed to help us. We had only a few minutes to save anything in the house.

As we were all gathered there in the area in front of the house, dad noticed I was barefoot. He had recently purchased me a new pair of shoes, so he ran around the back of the house to retrieve them.

Because of the speed of the fire and heat, the whole roof was engulfed in flames, and the south side of the house started to collapse to the ground leaving just about one room standing at the back of the house. My mother asked me to go and check if dad was okay.

I ran to the back of the house and peeked through the only window left. And there I could see him standing in the center of what was left of the room, with my shoes in his hand, staring straight ahead above me as if he didn't see me.

Stopping his escape was a beam lying across in front of him that had caught on fire. I could not see any way possible for him to get out of there. I couldn't see how he could tolerate the heat of the flames surrounding him. Immediately, I ran back and alerted mom. Everyone hugged and prayed for him to be saved.

In an instant, that one and final room collapsed with a loud "Whoosh," and he was standing outside, facing in the direction we were standing, looking toward us.

I believe Jesus accompanied him in the flames. Similar to the time the fourth man Jesus was present in the fire with the

Hebrew children. In addition, the amazing thing, besides the other perils, is that the collapsing building didn't fall on him. He only had a slight scratch on his arm, and not a hair on his head was burned. This led me to think of the fourth man in the fire with Shadrach, Meshach, and Abednego, where, bound in flames, the king commanded that they should heat the furnace one seven times more than it was wont to be heated. Daniel 3:19,

"The king saw four men loose, walking in the midst of the fire, and they have no hurt; and the form of the fourth is like the Son of God."

I almost forgot to tell you, I got my new shoes, and they had no scars or burns on them either.

"We are giving an emphatic thank you to our Lord and Savior Jesus, the.fourth man in the.fire!"

(Daniel 3:13-27)

Now that we were all safe with nowhere known to go as we had available for us to stay, word reached us that there was a house in the vicinity, down the gravel road, and it was vacant. The next step was to contact the owner. That house saved us from being homeless. The next amazing thing was the low rent at just $5 dollars a month.

I heard the owner was a beekeeper who we had met previously. He and his wife had a home only a few miles away from ours.

We became good friends after the incident. Thank you, Jesus!

Jesus Christ is Our Lord and Savior

Soon after the fire, we moved. Our dad went to California, got a job, and asked us to join him there, and we did. We had family living there, a cousin with her husband and an aunt, so we felt 'right at home' upon arrival.

As time passed, we soon got jobs and joined a church near our residence. My first job there was working at a laundry within walking distance of our home. I found favor with the owner, who had a mobile home attached to the building.

One day he needed some supplies, so he told me to go to the trailer and tell his wife to give me the keys to his car and use them to get the items needed from the store. Now, I had never met his wife, and he was sending me to get the keys to his car from her?

I was expecting her to be hesitant handing the keys to a stranger, but I suppose he must have told her about me and how I showed much interest in all areas of the production there; she immediately handed me the keys. After that, I started working all the dryers, hanging the military life preserver jackets in the drying room, and studying the washers and sewing machines.

Those life preservers were used on the navy vessels and were delivered to the shipyard for loading onto the ships. One day the person assigned to deliver the load of life preserver jackets became ill and couldn't make the delivery, so who do you think got the opportunity to do so? Me!

As the truck was parked there, waiting to take a load to the ship, the boss came to me and told me what needed to be done. He informed me that the ship was scheduled to receive this load and would leave soon, so the load had to be there today.

He directed me to get into the truck and show him that I knew how to change the gears. This was necessary because it was not an automatic transmission but a "stick" shift. I showed him that it was no problem for me, so he gave me permission to go and take that load away.

I left there, drove to the shipyard from Oakland to San Francisco, and somehow arrived at the correct location. I met someone there who guided me in backing the truck up to the appropriate dock to unload. He told me that dinner was being served on the ship, and I should go in and eat while they unloaded the truck. So, I went in and saw they were serving chicken chowmein for the meal. I didn't even know what that was until I ate it and enjoyed it. Even now, I still like chowmein.

I felt good being able to do all that I got to do at age 19. 'To be respected, trusted, and given tasks that would normally be given to a seasoned adult, someone who would be so much older than me in years of age.

The owner selected me to be the one to do all deliveries of clothing to businesses and life preservers to ships in San Francisco.

Again, all the praise to God, our Father, through Christ Jesus, our Lord, and Savior.

Before we left Arkansas, the recruiters had been trying to get me enlisted into the Armed Forces, so as soon as I arrived in California, the Selective Service started contacting me regularly, and I kept ignoring them. It was not very long before two men who had just been discharged from the Army began coming to our house to see my sisters. They appeared to be above my age, and I didn't ask their age, but having completed two years of military service I knew they had to be several years older than me. My sisters told their friends that I didn't want to go into the Army and that I had been throwing the letters received into the trash. Their friends informed me that there may be unfavorable consequences if I didn't answer those greeting letters.

Before I received another one, I went to the recruiting office and joined the Army.

I was only going to do 2 years and quit; however, I found favor with the Cadre and the Lord once I was into my training assignment. The person performing the training activities thought I had been a prior service person seeing my actions within the company and started treating me as a cadre even though I had not had any prior service in the Military. They put me and another person who served in the national guard in charge of the ongoing activities. So, I was treated as one of them.

After completing basic training in California, I was sent to Texas, where I was also treated as Cadre. While there, I sustained a leg injury on a field trip and got blood poising. I was taken to the hospital for treatment and immediately passed out. I woke up 3 days later at the sound of the doctors standing by my bed talking about me needing some serious surgery, but before they could schedule me for it, I was miraculously healed and discharged. I felt so good that I went to the other patient's beds and wished them the wellness I had received. Some had been in that hospital for as long as 18 months and with no expectation of leaving anyway soon.

After advanced training, I was sent overseas by ship on the Atlantic Ocean. We encountered a bad storm that had the ship rocking 23 degrees or more. All the passengers got very sick in that situation except one other person and me. Again, thanks to our Lord and Savior, Jesus! He watches over those who trust him even when you don't think he is present.

I was there only a few days before I got a promotion and was put in charge of people again. Some thought it was because

I was against them and began to call me a 'Cheese Eater' but again, it was from the Lord. Nothing special that I had done or thought that I had done. Soon after that being only Private First Class, I was selected to attend the Non-Commissioned Officers Academy, where we had a commander's inspection. All were eliminated except a Master Sergeant with a lot of military experience and medals, and me. I had nothing but my one little stripe, and he had many.

The commander stood there for a long time looking back and forth at both when finally, he raised his arm and brought it down, pointing to the Master Sergeant as the winner. He was so impressed with me that he wrote a letter of commendation to my unit commander for a special recommendation. So again, the Lord gets the glory for the things he has done.

As time passed, I had guard duty where one could be selected to be what is called the 'Colonel's Orderly' which netted you a three-day pass. Every time I appeared at the inspection, I was selected and eventually received so many 3-day passes that I never used them all, not even on my tour there in Germany.

Now on one of those passes, I went to a village, as was our usual custom to go, where one could meet very nice people and enjoy some good food and drinks. Unfortunately, one time, I got stuck in the little town. I went to the bus station to return to my unit location, but only the attendant was there, told me that the last bus for the day had departed and there would not be another until 8:00am the next day.

It was about 10:00 pm, and it was getting very cold. Too cold for the summer clothes that I was wearing. I kept wondering where I was going to stay until the next day. Surely, not outside, and I couldn't stay at the bus station.

I proceeded to walk along the road with houses on both sides of it. I came across two dimly lit houses, one on the right side near me and one on the left side, several houses farther down the road. I took the chance for the closest because my legs were so cold that I could barely walk. I was convinced I wouldn't make it if I kept walking any longer. I had to approach whoever lived in this house and pray they would receive me.

I went to the first house, walked up the porch to the door, and knocked. I heard footsteps coming toward the door. I wondered how to explain my situation because it was getting late, and I didn't want the door to be closed right in front of me.

The door opened, and there appeared a woman who looked to be about forty years of age. I quickly introduced myself and explained to her that I went to the bus station to get a bus to my camp and found no more buses were leaving until morning. Then I asked if I could come in and stay until then, and with the look on her face and her holding the door tightly, I immediately let her know I would not bother her and that I could sleep right here by the door on the floor.

It was then that I saw her countenance change greatly. She looked relieved, opened the door all the way, let me in, and in a frail voice said, "I can't let you sleep on the floor, but there on that raised section level, you may sleep in my daughter's bed because she is no longer here."

"You will have to leave early in the morning because I must go to work." She informed me, and I agreed.

She went to the rear area of the house while I got to bed and lay there thinking how great the Lord Jesus is. A total stranger found a house to escape the cold through a woman who was no longer afraid of me being there all night. Would I have let a stranger into my home after 10:00 pm in the dark of night? *I don't think so.*

The following day, she arrived at my bedside with a smile and a plate of food and said to me, "As soon as you finish eating this, it will be time to leave because I have to be getting to work."

I was greatly surprised to be receiving this pleasant treatment so soon. That really made me feel the Lord in all of this. I ate the food, left for the bus station, and was on time. Then I thought, perhaps I should have taken the plate back to her but left well enough as it is.

After my gun section the chief retired, I got another promotion and became Gun Section Chief. We had these big guns and moved them to a place for target practice on the Baltic Sea. It was there that my section won first place over the many sections that we had there in our organization. I didn't think of me being special as I was just doing what I was supposed to do. Talk about favor after favor, even when I didn't think I deserved it.

After about three and a half years at this one assignment in Germany, I received orders to the United States. I was transported by ship and arrived in the City of New York. Later, I was put on a train to my assignment in Michigan. I was going to Sault Saint Marie, which was in the Upper Peninsula, not knowing what actions or directions would be happening on the way there.

It seemed we would never get there as they made occasional stops. I kept periodically asking the conductor, "Are we there yet?"

He kept saying, "Don't worry, I will let you know when we get there."

I wish he had said, "You'll know because the train will be at the end of the track and can go no further."

Finally, we arrived, and I notified the organization that I needed someone to give me a ride to my assigned location. Soon the transportation arrived, and I got to see where I would be stationed for the next year and a half. That was also the time I had left for my military tour.

This is where I met my soon-to-be wife. As soon as we got to know each other, I told her, "I'm taking you home with me."

I don't know if she believed me, but she just smiled and kept walking. So that was as good as a prophecy because it really happened, and we have been together now for 62 years plus.

Unfortunately, she passed away before I could complete writing this. Her loss is the most difficult thing I have ever had to endure in my life so far. She was such a wonderful person helping me and others always. The only thing that sustains me is that she accepted our Lord and Savior, Jesus, years ago, and I know she is with him now because we have his word on it.

Before we left Michigan, some more things happened in the spirit realm that I and others could bear witness to. This one happened on an evening as I returned to my assignment. We had a fence surrounding the place and a guard on duty at our communications 'Bubble,' as we called it, because of the look of it with the clear rise on the top where one could see the sky above.

It so happened that the guard on duty that evening was the younger of almost all of us there, but he talked slowly as a much older person and seemed to know much more of life than all of us there. In fact, we used to say that he sounded like a real old man. So, as I arrived at the locked gate that evening, this person on guard duty was the same person who was slow in the movement and came running toward the gate, screaming and pointing back toward the Bubble. I looked up there and saw this huge spaceship hovering over the Bubble.

Don't worry about my discernment of a spaceship because I was already familiar with them. My sisters and I had seen them when we were children in Arkansas, and there was another one in Germany, which you have most likely seen the video on television. These vehicles are real.

I don't even remember if he opened the gate for me because, by the time he arrived at the gate after setting a speed record running away from that hovering vehicle, I saw it leaving slowly and heading toward another one of our sites. I immediately decided to rush there to warn them, but as slow as it had left our location, it beat me there even as fast as I was going.

I arrived just in time to see it hovering over their Bubble, and all the personnel there were running around as in an emergency preparation for whatever was to happen.

The next thing I remembered was that I was supposed to go to my fiancé's house, but I could not go for a while because my car wouldn't start until that spaceship was clear of the area. So, after that, my car starts easily, and I proceeded to her house and picked her up as planned.

We were married while I was still in Michigan and deciding what to do with my military career after I told her, *"I am taking you home with me."*

We finally decided to go to California and take some time away to make the lasting decision of going back and finishing my career in the service of my country or taking the civilian route. We decided to go to the military again.

Now, the next big event was that I reentered military service and began to see spiritual activity more than before in my life. My first assignment was to go to Fort Bliss, Texas. While there, I could get assigned to a location in California, so I left my wife there to work it out; however, that fell through. So, I returned to Oakland, picked her up and returned to Texas.

While on a field training exercise, I injured my leg again and was admitted to the same hospital as before. This time I was married, and my wife visited me regularly. Finally, I got a new assignment to a new station in Washington and received orders for an assignment to Korea. We left the west coast by ship, leaving my wife in Oakland and sailing through under the Golden Gate Bridge. Then, I felt separated from the United States as we were moving slowly on smooth water.

After getting to a point about halfway across the ocean, we were informed that a storm was coming over us. After all of that beautiful sunshine, a storm?

We checked the deck periodically to see if all was well when we got word that 50- foot waves were starting to come toward us. So, I decided to make one more check on the deck, and as I went up the steps, unlocked and opened the door, I noticed it didn't look too bad. I could barely see the ship's forward deck because of the darkness, so I stepped out, turned, and locked the door behind me, then turned to look forward toward the front of the ship. I took a step forward, and the big wave hit as if it were planned just for me.

It was dark, and even with one small light on the ship above me, I couldn't see past the side rails of the ship. Then, suddenly, I was thrown straight up above the deck as this huge wave hit. I estimate I went as much as 30 feet or more above the ship's deck when it started going straight down, leaving me floating in mid-air. A soft, warm blanket of hot air engulfed me, holding me suspended there with the ship going down, down, down, far away from me.

I started to wonder if the ship was sinking because it looked as if it wouldn't stop going down, and the wave that hit sounded like an explosion. In this horizontal position that I was in, warm and relaxed, stretched out facing down, I folded my arms.

I said, "I will just wait here until it comes back up."

As if l could do anything of myself to make sure that it comes back up. Whoa, this thing is not coming back up but staying down and turning slowly to my right. Why?

While all this was happening, I noticed that I was staying in the air and drifting all the way over the side rail. Just as I am perfectly positioned over the rail, the ship is now coming back up while I am still horizontal and facing down. That is why I could see the rail so well and the blackness of the ocean beyond it.

No fear could enter because I felt comfortable until I was flipped over onto my back and hit that rail hard. After landing on the rail very hard and knowing that I was only inches from going into the ocean if I went to my left or onto the steel deck if I went to my right. I went to my right, sliding onto the ship's deck. I realized I had no control over whether I went overboard into the ocean side of that rail or if I went off onto the ship's deck.

Immediately I slid down onto the ship's deck. The Lord directed my landing. I suppose I was turned over onto my back to avoid seeing where I was in the alignment of that ship's railing.

l praise you forever, Lord and savior Jesus. for your divine protection and grace!

I felt no pain with the hard landing on that railing or the steel deck. Immediately I got up and rushed to that door to open it and get back inside as fast as possible before the next huge wave hit. It wasn't very long before we arrived at our destination in Korea.

"How shall we escape, if we neglect so great salvation, which at first began to be spoken by the Lord and was confirmed unto us by them that heard him. "

(Hebrews 2: 3)

The next event occurred while I was stationed in Korea on a field training exercise. After completing that training session, two other people and I were tasked with getting one of our trucks back to the camp location ahead of the next convoy. Having been up for such a long time without sleep, all three of us were very sleepy. While moving along the road safely, we started falling asleep. To stop that element, we started beating each other on the shoulder with our fists and still went to sleep.

We were on a straight way on the road when we started bouncing roughly in the vehicle and noticed that we were off the road and into a ditch. Then, we noticed that the trailer we were towing had turned over. Finally, as we were sitting in the vehicle thinking about how to set the trailer back upright, we noticed the top Commanding Officer sitting on the road right beside us.

Our first thought was, "Boy, are we in trouble."

Much to our surprise, he only asked if we were all right. We let him know we were okay and would set the trailer back up and head home. He left without further comment. We did get out of the truck, and the three of us set the trailer up and proceeded on the road.

The big thing about this is not running off the road there in that small ditch but that we were wide awake and prepared for the serious portion of the trip. Just a little way up ahead of us was a steep hill, or you could even say a cliff that we used to joke about going around the curve at high altitude with two of the wheels in the air floating on nothing. Think about what would or could have happened had we gone to sleep and driven off at that location. So, you see, I believe we ran off the road to ensure that we were wide awake at that most dangerous location just ahead of us.

To God be the glory for what he has done for us through our Lord and savior, Jesus.

After returning from Korea, I proceeded to my assignment at Fort Sill, Oklahoma. It wasn't long before we had to travel to Germany on a huge training mission. After completion of the specified time limit of the training, we were set to return to our assigned location at Fort Sill. As we loaded onto the airplane, we noticed that we had a big load, but we didn't see any problem until we started moving to lift-off.

After 3 attempts and many prayers, we were in the air and very happy that we had made it. Praise be to our Lord Jesus! While we were over the ocean, one of the 4 engines stopped running. Then another stopped, but we were told the pilot had done this on purpose, so everyone kept talking as if no problem existed. Later the third engine stopped. Now there is much concern because how will we stay airborne when we had a slight problem on lift-off from the runway with 4 engines, and now with only one engine running?

Soon, the plane was descending toward the ocean with only 1 engine running. That made it tilt to the opposite side, and with the long wingspan, one of the wings was heading toward the water. It became quiet in the plane as all were praying again and looking at a wing tip that seemed to be about 10 feet from making contact with the ocean. At what one would call the last second the engine on that side started. We were level again but at a low altitude.

Not so bad, but there sits the mountain right in front of us, and we have to climb to an altitude that will clear it. That means to me we need all 4 engines again to pull up in time, and through Jesus and much prayer from our wives at home, and us, we got it done. Thanks are to the Lord, our God.

We had to hold off the landing when we cleared the mountain because a smaller plane had crashed, and the runway needed clearing. As soon as it was cleared, we landed. It wasn't long after that we were able to return home to Fort Sill. My wife was always praying for my safety.

The next event I want to mention is when I was chosen to attend computer school at Fort Sill, Oklahoma. While attending, we decided to help the Officer Candidate Students from the current attrition rate by forming an Officer Candidate Preparation School. Again, there I was selected, not volunteer. Now I could believe that my steps were the order of the Lord. I was very pleased to be selected to help set up this school and put forth my best effort to make it successful.

As we proceeded with task accomplishment, we had to watch the students comply with instructions. One of the requirements was that the students leave their wives and automobiles at home because of the time factors for what had to be done; both would be a hindrance. Wouldn't you know it, one of the students brought both his wife and car, a Supercar, one of those huge engines with wide "fat tires" on the rear axle; a "Hot Rod" by definition.

One day, after the Post Commander had moved his office to a place right across the street from ours, this person, not knowing it, laid about a 3-block strip of rubber onto the pavement right in front of that office. I was told that the commander called for his appearance before him.

21

This is to be continued because something good came out of this. This person conformed and became a student who graduated from both the OCS Prep School and the Officers Candidate School to become a helicopter pilot in our organization in Vietnam. I got to watch his action there, too and witness that he was well equipped for military service. More on this later.

Several of our cadres got Vietnam assignments as we continued training OCS Prep Students. Then finally, I was sent there too. First, I reported to Oakland, California, to prepare for the assignment, which included a group orientation. While we were participating in the final speech, the person presenting it paused, scanned the group slowly, and said, "Some of you will not be coming back."

Immediately I aborted that statement by saying, "I'm coming back." Then, after I had time to think of nothing in particular, I said, "but if I don't, I am taking 5 of them with me."

I did not realize how dumb it was to make that unnecessary statement.

Picture this now. We have just arrived in Vietnam on this civilian aircraft. Right after exiting the airplane, we gathered to listen to the person responsible for giving us our assigned locations. A gun fired, passing a bullet right between our heads. Our comment was.

"What the h*ll was that?"

The Cadre said that it was a usual occurrence.

We said, "Why doesn't someone go and eliminate him?"

The answer was to do that. In Cadre's words, "You may get a great shooter who will hit all of us; This one never hits anybody."

With that said, we started concentrating on where we were going from there. The very next day, I was taken to a place where one could get his weapon oriented to hit what was aimed at and planned to hit. This person told me that there should be people on the site already. Upon arrival, after driving through many wooded areas and watching the driver leaning over the steering wheel and looking left and right as if expecting ambush, we stopped in the clearing and saw no one. This person told me there should be people on the site already, so I got out of the truck for a better look around the area. Immediately, the truck driver took off and left me standing there. I thought, what if no one shows up, and I am left here to go back walking through those woods alone? After all, there is fighting going on here.

I waited for some time, thinking about why I didn't stay in the truck so he couldn't run off and leave me standing there like this. While a hundred thoughts ran through my head, I realized this was not the firing range in the US, where I had spent many days on my own. I noticed a huge bush there shaking violently, causing me to prepare for the worst. It wasn't long before I saw the first person step out of that cluster of bushes, then another and another, until there were about 10 people there. Somehow, I trusted the uniforms and didn't fire on them. We started firing our weapons at the targets available without exchanging any dialogue.

As we were planning our walk back to camp, a bullet passed between us, causing us to hit the ground. When we got up, we started talking about how we got so low we had to look up to see the grass. I think someone said the grassroots must have had a laugh. On our walk back, we spread out, forming two columns and made a safe trip back to camp. As soon as we were back at camp, a convoy was ready to go to the northern areas of the assignment.

My first plan was to ride up front to see the areas we were to pass through, so I did. As we passed through a place known for ambushes, the rear of the convoy was hit. The next time I was on another convoy going the same direction, I took the rear location, and the front was hit. The front had a friendly military unit operating there that handled that ambush. I never learned what happened to the rear attack we had before.

Getting back to the "More on this later" part, one night, as I had left the operations to get some rest, I received a call to report back to my assigned location because an officer there wanted to see me. My first thought was that I must have made a mistake in procedures and was in trouble. The officer who wanted to see me was our assigned helicopter pilot- His father was stationed in the area well south of us. He had come up to see me because his son, our pilot, had told him so many great things about me from our training of him in the US; remember the "Supercar hotrod."

Again, I don't want to take credit for my praise, but give glory to God, our Father, through Jesus, our Lord and savior.

After being at this location, we were required to move further North and set up a new location. Upon arrival, we conferred with the officer in charge as he stood there looking at a 7-foot hole dug by an enemy rocket. We asked where he wanted us to set up the operations center. Without speaking a word, he simply raised his arm with his index finger pointing down to the center of that big hole. We enquired if he was joking and found that he was not. He simply said this location would never be hit again. He must have had some input from above because that location was never hit, even though some hits came close.

One Sunday, as it was quiet, the other officer in charge decided to step out of the bunker built for us and see the sunshine for a change. He had only got to the one opening in the bunker, stopped and beckoned us to come to see what he saw; a heavy mortar aimed at that opening which could have been sealed and held all of us in there. He sent our Helicopter pilot out, the one I told you about before, and that threat was immediately eliminated. Talk about timing, last minute. I see Jesus in this. Some say last-minute, but I see him always being on time.

On another occasion, we moved from that location and were on another assignment. As we could not land solid onto the ground due to the steep angle of the area, we had to jump off the helicopter on the downhill side. I fell and found myself rolling downhill, injuring my already problematic leg. As soon as I was up, I received word that the Red Cross needed me at base camp. I was able to fly back by helicopter to take care of that situation. On my way returning to the field area, I had to go to another place by truck, and jumping off that tall truck added to the injury.

I had to stay at that place overnight because there was no transportation to leave there. While there, I met a person I had served besides in the United States. I was going to lie down for the night on well-soaked wet grass when he told me I could use his canvas cot as he had to leave there on a mission. The next morning, one other person and I were told to stand out at a special place to get on a helicopter coming in, only to find it was a medical aircraft. This aircraft came in fast and stopped to let us onboard. As soon as we boarded, I noticed a medic giving artificial resuscitation to someone on the floor behind the main seats. I was unaware of who that was at the time.

The first stop was at a field tent, where we unloaded and went in to see the physician. While there, I was standing beside a stretcher with a patient on it. The person tending him had his back turned toward the patient and facing a bench where he was working on what appeared to be a motor of some sort. While we were waiting to talk to him, this person on the gurney, uncovered from the waistline up to his head, started turning dark blue all over his skin up to the hair on his head. I don't know how the doctor knew it, but he swiftly moved into action.

What he did really moved me. He took the blade there and stabbed this person in the right side of the chest, then shoved a clear tube into the opening and turned the motor on connected to the attached tubing. Immediately, fluid started flowing from the chest cavity through that tube, and the skin started returning to the normal color, and that person lived. I thought, wow. What a doctor.

The next thing that happened was that he told us there was no room for us, so we had to get back onto the helicopter and proceed to the next location.

As soon as we left, I noticed that we were headed straight out over the South China Sea. Now, I am wondering how much fuel we have as this aircraft has been running for quite some time, and now, we are over a very large body of water. After going a long distance, I noticed a white object that looked about the size of a normal white bar of soap out in the middle of the sea. Shortly after, we could see it was a medical ship because of the red cross.

We landed on that ship and saw it was truly a medical ship. We went downstairs into the hall and met with a doctor who took the injured person into the first room right off the hallway. After a few minutes, he informed us that the person had passed away. At that moment, I finally found that he was the person I had served with and had given me that cot to use and avoid the wet grass when he went on a special mission. What made me feel alright was the idea that he was now with Jesus, and we still had to think about what would happen next.

After being on that hospital ship for a few days and being able to walk a bit, dragging my right leg, I would go to the upper deck daily and look toward the jungle, thinking about what was going on there and praying for it to change. One day, the action got heavy, and some of the injured were brought to the ship. The commander told me that some room had to be made, which meant everyone who could walk had to evacuate. In preparation to leave the ship, I walked by the room that had just received two of the wounded. The first one appeared to be expired, missing all limbs. I thought I would give up my space gladly for them. As I approached the next one, he appeared to be the enemy. He rose and started shaking. It was then that I could see his serious wound, so I turned away quickly and proceeded to the exit door.

I climbed down the net into the vehicle that was to take us to shore. It was high powered and loud. There appeared to be four persons on it; the driver, me, and two others. To me, this meant that three of us would leave the ship and return to our units. No words were ever spoken between us. We soon arrived on shore, and as I attempted to get off the boat, my stiff leg caught the rim, spun me around, and fell on my back to the ground. I saw no one there but me and the boat operator. Immediately, the boat operator gave it full throttle, heading back to the ship. I laid there on my back, watching the boat until it appeared to have returned to where the ship was and shutting the motor off. I couldn't see it there because it was so small, and I could barely see the ship's silhouette.

My first thought was, "You dummy. Get up and get moving. You are in Vietnam, where anyone you know of out after dark alone was no more."

I crawled up to the ridgeline and started scanning the open area between the sea and the tree line and estimating the distance from the water's edge to the tree line where I was planning to hide and work out a way to survive and look for my assigned unit. I had consumed no food, just a small amount of water in my canteen.

I examined the grass's height and noticed that it was not tall enough to hide anyone there. I remembered there is another problem called "spider holes." I planned to get into the tree line, find a bush to hide in and listen for sounds, and by early morning be prepared to move from that location and continue looking for friendly forces. I thought about the person I first met that took me to the firing range. He was the first person I knew who was found with multiple stab wounds after being away from friendly forces, just as I am now.

I got up and started walking across that open area. Again, the same thought entered my mind, and I started thinking that if anyone was here, they must have heard that loud boat and knew it had brought someone to shore. As I approach the middle of the clear area halfway between the sea and the tree line, I see these five figures coming up and surrounding me in a 12-hour clock-face fashion. My first thought then was, "Uh,

27

Oh." I started picturing my wife reading a newspaper titled "Man Missing In Action." But wait, didn't I say, "I'm coming back" when the chaplain said, "Some of you won't be coming back." The next thing I added to it was, "If I don't, I'm taking five of them with me." See how your mind can work in times of serious consequences.

Here I was surrounded by five, and I had an urgent thought and the sound of a voice telling me I have got to find which one was the leader because there has to be a leader. As soon as I heard this voice, instead of just a thought, I noticed the two near the 2 pm hour on the clock face that I was seeing started to separate. The one nearest to the 12-noon space moved to exactly in the 12- noon spot, right in front of me.

All of them were closing in on me, and I had no weapons to fight with. Retrospectively. It was a good thing because I probably would have lost the battle. The one in front of me started approaching me with this large blade he held in his right hand, pointing toward me.

I heard the voice of the Lord say,

"Don't look at the blade. Look at his eyes only and nothing else."

And that is what I did.

Now, he was right in front of me and shoved that blade into contact with my chest. I kept my eyes looking straight into his eyes, and he into my eyes. He shoved the blade

firmer into my chest, and I did not change my expression. Next, he shoved that blade hard into my chest, making it feel like it had now broken the skin. I remembered what I was told to do. I held that position even though I really wanted to go right through this person barehanded.

I even heard myself thoughtfully saying, "Why doesn't he get out of my way? Doesn't he know I have to be in that tree line before sundown?"

I believe that strange questioning kept me still and prevented me from doing something stupid. Holding that blade in my chest, this person rose onto his toes, looking weirdly into my eyes as if looking down through a tunnel and wondering why I was showing no fear or making an attempt to fight back.

The next thing he did while still holding that blade to my chest was to lean over a bit toward my left shoulder, looking past me, and with my peripheral vision, I could see that the persons who were still at the 2 pm and the 10 am positions were all looking in the same direction beyond me. My first thought was this was a diversion to force me into a move so they could finish me off. Little did I know it was JESUS because as soon as they looked, their eyes showed fear. As if a gun was fired in a competitive racing match, all five of them started running as fast as they could, gathering shoulder to shoulder and going south of where we had been standing.

I stood there watching them until they were going out of sight, as I could only see their heads bobbing now due to the curvature of the field and they were still running fast. I turned to see what they had seen to spark that much fear in them, causing them to run like that, but I saw nothing. Then, I knew it had been the LORD who protects me. Now, I also knew my next move was to get to that tree line and hide, but as I walked that way, I thought, I can't stay near this location. What if they come back? I almost forgot to mention that I still have a bump on my chest bone even now where that blade struck me. I think that blade must be what caused the bump.

As I arrived at the tree line, I saw those cartwheel tracks usually made by buffalo drawn carts. I decided to follow them but not to the right because that is where those men went. The only way then is to go to the left, which is what I did. I quickly arrived at a dirt road and, to my surprise, met a military vehicle. Talk about precision timing. *The LORD JESUS is perfect.*

That driver had his mouth and eyes wide open. He stopped and said to me, "What are you doing out here? Are you trying to get yourself killed?"

I told him I had just gotten off the hospital ship and was trying to find my assigned unit. I didn't tell him about the ordeal that I had just been delivered out of. He told me about some friendly people's appearance he had seen along the way and offered to take me back there. I got into the vehicle, and we proceeded to arrive where he had seen them. On the way there, I thought about the two people I had been stationed with that were in the same type of vehicle and were destroyed by the direct hit of a rocket. I was hoping that wouldn't happen to us.

I got out of the vehicle and walked up to the person near me, introduced myself, and let him know the name of the unit that I was looking for, then asked if he had seen this unit that I was assigned to, but he had not. Before I could feel stuck there, he turned and let me know that is a helicopter down the hill there going to base camp.

I hurried to get there and simultaneously met the pilot on his way to the helicopter. I asked if it was okay to ride with him. He simply told me to hop in. Talk about being right on time again and again with JESUS. First, the deliverance from my enemy who had me surrounded. Then, the Military vehicle could have passed me up had we not arrived at a location at the same time. Finally, the helicopter leaving for base camp. That's 3 salvations in a row.

The first thing I noticed were the bullet holes in the canopy right in front of me sitting in the seat of that helicopter. I spent the trip hoping none of those were put there again. Upon arrival at base camp, I remembered that the doctor who had attended me on the hospital ship had told me to see a doctor when I returned to my unit before taking any serious action. I saw the doctor there at base camp immediately, and after examining me, he told me I was to stay there until my condition improved. As I was there for a few days, the officer in charge of the camp had the person assigned to give orientations to the people headed for a return to the United States to pass the task to me.

I had only given one presentation when the commander had a different assignment for me because the R and R (Rest and Recuperation) Detachment leader was leaving too. He placed me into that position, a much larger job than just giving orientations to personnel returning to the United States of America. I went to the Detachment location and picked a place to stay in one of the buildings close to my place of duty. Having a lot of papers to read concerning the operations, I wanted to be in a quiet location because the people coming off the battlefield action were very noisy.

To do this, I had to move all the way up to the end of the building arrangements. This put me up near the wooded area, or jungle, as we called it. The first time up there, I say up there because it was an uphill walk to get there. I went into the building and saw about 24 cots there with mattresses rolled up on them and the area empty otherwise. I chose the third bunk from the door in case someone decided to fight me, I would have a little distance to get set to protect myself.

As I was sitting there on the bunk reading the instructions I was given, and with my back toward the door (not a smart move), just before sundown, I heard this strange sound. I tensed my muscles and looked toward the window on the tree line side, thinking perhaps it was the enemy, and again I had no weapon. It had a partly hissing and sharp sound mixed like a short hiss mixed with a sneeze air sound. This is very difficult to describe like a sound I had never heard before. There was a loud echo in the building as this is a metal open building with a concrete floor. The second time it did this, I knew it was in the building where I was sitting and between me and the door, but when I looked, I saw nothing. I waited a few seconds, and this time the same sound was under the bunk that I was sitting on.

This meant I better look under the bunk to see what this was. I slowly began to move, only my upper body bending over while keeping my feet still to see what was there. As my eyes passed the bed frame, I was expecting to see a small furry 4-legged

31

creature. To my surprise, it was a bamboo viper coiled about 2 inches from my bare leg, preparing to strike me. A deadly reptile that I had heard so much about is called the one-step snake. That is all you get to take if it bites you, then you are dead. I was just staring at it mesmerized, as it appeared to be deciding which skin pore to hit, when it suddenly popped its head around to stare at me, and it was staring back with a hateful look in its eyes.

After a while in this position, I heard the voice of the LORD say to me very solidly, "as soon as he breaks vision with you, he is going to strike ... Move!" Now my intellect gets into the way and thinks, if that is the LORD why is he calling it he instead of it? Immediately I got my answer. "Because to you, it is not vicious. This one is very vicious!" My plan was to simply jerk my feet up and lie back on the bed while I figured out what to do, as we both cannot stay in this place at the same time tonight.

This did not happen because as soon as the word move was spoken, I shot straight up toward the ceiling at a high speed, poised in military attention fashion, with my arms pinned straight down to my sides with no bend in my arms or legs and my head almost reached the ceiling. I paused there a second and thought that if I went back straight down where my feet were before, he could still bite me. However, I did not go back down but was moved backward while still in the air to what had to be the perfect center of the bed. Then, I was let down onto the bed.

Again, we talk about the last minute. How about perfection as I was let down into what I believe had to be the perfect center of that bed? This is how I knew the LORD was directing my actions because I could not have done those movements myself.

Praise yet the LORD: **Psalm 150:1-6**

My next move was to find something to eliminate this critter from this building, so I am standing there with the springs sagging and probably hitting the head of the coiled viper under the bed. I scan the whole room and finally see a straw wooden handle broom way away at the far end. This is as perfect as it gets under the circumstances because the straws are worn off to the binding material making this the perfect "shovel" to accomplish the task at hand.

I had to figure out the best angle to leap from where I was standing to the isle between the bunk beds and land on the run. I could land on the next bunk if the angle is too sharp. If too flat, I could kick the bed backward from under me and land on the enemy because the steel bunk was not anchored to the concrete floor. When I had the exact plan in mind, I leaped, landed perfectly into the aisle, and ran to the end of the building where I saw the broom stored. I grabbed it and spun around to see if I had been followed. I had not been followed as he was just out from under the bed now, but still, even with it coiled in the isle between the bunks in the full coiled strike position, ready to fight me.

I started my return approach for the showdown and planned to first get this critter to uncoil, then take the broom handle and beat him to death. He outdrew me as I made my quickdraw approach and caught him in the middle of the back just as he made his strike for me, which was halfway between the head and the tail. Immediately, the violent repetitious striking began, pow! pow! pow! I counted over 25 strikes, each one getting about an eighth of an inch closer to my bare toe as I kept this one pinned to the floor, or so I thought.

The sound was awful and loud in this mostly empty metal and concrete building, sounding much like a rifle firing. At this time, I thought this thing would beat his brains out, hitting the concrete floor this hard. By now, it was within one-eighth of an inch of my big toe on my right foot, meaning that with one more strike, he would hit my toe.

Now the LORD is on the scene because he stopped striking, leaned over to look past me, and showed fear in his eyes just as the men who had me surrounded in the field. I thought this might be a diversion to get me to move, but then he tore out from under that broom I held and headed for the open door.

I noticed that the door was standing open about a foot wide. With the bunks blocking a good hit, I would have to wait until we get near the door for a space wide enough to get the hit crosswise the body to be effective as he attempts to exit through the door. The problem now was that he turned away to the side from the door and accessed the louvers between the boards at the bottom of the wall forcing his head between them and splitting them open, making a loud crack sound that echoed through the building again and forcing a way through them. I thought I could hold him with a broom. I decided to let go of the situation as I figured anything that left me with that much fear would never return.

I closed the door and sat on the bed, and immediately there was a knock. I could not understand who could be knocking because I had just looked and saw no one. And, when I came up to this place, I watched to see that no one was seeing me choose to be up here. l opened the door, and much to my surprise, there stood two men who looked almost like twins in statues and dressed in what we call "class A" uniforms.

I had not seen anyone dressed in anything but jungle fatigues or black pajamas or the North Vietnam Army uniform over there. The next thing I noticed was no evidence of shaving on the smooth facial skin. One of them was holding a brand-new galvanized steel bucket. He said to me a few words in a language I had to pick words, and I got two of them, the word "look" and "death," and as I leaned over the bucket to look, I saw these viper vertebrae I had just dealt with. How I knew it was him because the mouth had a spot of flesh left on the burned remains coiled inside the bucket. How could this possibly happen in only a few seconds? One could see that there had been a very hot blue flame in that bucket, and yet, the vertebrae were clean and in perfect shape as it could ever be. But it was not burned, and there were no ashes in the bucket.

I just stood there looking at the one on the right, then the one on the left, then into the bucket, so amazed that I couldn't speak, and they never said another word. And where does one get a brand-new galvanized steel bucket there with no stores to sell them, and how could a hot flame be started that soon and remove all flesh except a small portion on the mouth? This went on for a while. Finally, they looked at each other, turned, and left, walking toward the woods. I watched them, wondering why they were walking so slowly, as if to see if I would get the notion to call them back for discussion. And why were they headed into the woods in "Dress" uniforms instead of going down the beaten path leading to the office building or other areas, after all, dress uniforms? I didn't call them, but I wish I had talked with them now because I believe they are either my assigned Angels or those assigned for that specific occasion.

Upon returning from Vietnam, I went back to the unit I was with and continued teaching and processing students for Officer Candidate School. Soon, it was like the dust was still on my boots when I was called to Vietnam again. This time I went to a unit that worked from a fixed location. We still got enemy fire hurled at us but with no harm done. After about half of my tour there, based on assignments, some personnel were moved to new locations, while others were returned to the United States.

I was sent to a transportation unit to replace a person of my status in the military. With me, having been in the Field Artillery, he would remind me that you handle the convoy vehicles the same way as firing the projectiles from the big guns because all one had to do was "shoot 'em from here to there," as you would do with the big gun projectiles. However, the difference was that these vehicles came back at you. Good for laughs.

One day, as the convoy was leaving for the daily movement of the usual route, the commanding officer came into our operations center and said he had a problem and could not do his usual convoy monitoring with his helicopter. He told me to go and take his place with his pilot and watch the safe movement from the air. What? Me?

Take the place of a high-level commanding officer for convoy monitoring?

This has to be JESUS again. His pilot was already sitting out there with the motor running. Hence, as I approached the helicopter and told him what the commander had said, he gave me a curious look, wondering if I was telling him the truth or planning to hijack the helicopter.

Why not a Sergeant you never met taking the commanding officer's place in his helicopter to monitor the convoy? Finally, he said, "get in," and I did. As we had been enroute for a while, the pilot became sick because we were violently tossed about with updrafts, which never bothered me. I could see his skin changing color fast with a sickly look, so I asked if he wanted me to take the controls. Much to my surprise, he never asked if I was a pilot but simply said, "That's alright, I'll land for a few minutes and be okay."

We found a spot out between some fallen trees, landed, and got out of the helicopter. While sitting there in the trees, my thought was that be watchful for an ambush, but nothing happened. Later we returned to base camp safely.

Again, Praise and Bless the LORD Christ JESUS.

The next item to mention was when I returned to my same location in the US with a promotion enroute. I was back to teaching OCS Prep students. With a lot of combat experience on me, I can tell the students a lot about survival, I thought. One day, while on the usual field exercises, we were setting up for firing the weapons. Early that morning, I arrived at the site as it was our usual way of preparing for the students to arrive; I got it done by selecting kindling wood to start a fire in the little stove inside the building because it was cold.

This was done to allow for warm hands in using the slide rules and other equipment. Half of the students were inside the building, and the other half were outside to be forward observers. As I was in the front of the room, near the chalkboard, I decided to walk over to the window near me to see if they were ready outside to get started. As I turned to take the most direct route back to the chalkboard, I was almost against the wall when all of a sudden, I saw my mouth almost in contact 1,2,3,4,5,6,7 (seven rattlers hanging out of the wall).

I called out to the students, "Hey guys, look, there are 7 of them there." They looked, and as they did, I said, "If he doesn't bother me, I won't bother him." With that, we went to work. The data collection for the targets and the other equipment were all being prepared. As the students were doing their duties, I talked to them and pressed myself up against the first row of benches, which put me closer to the students since no one was sitting in the first row.

As I was giving my instructions, at about 9 am, the room was getting well warm. The students were busy looking down at their desktops and preparing the firing data. Then, all in unison, they looked up at my neck area with their mouths wide open as if to yell but said nothing. I immediately stopped talking and started my turn slowly to see what was going on. I remembered what was on the wall near the chalkboard. Only this time, they are looking at my neck. I decided to lean forward because I sensed they were looking at my neck, not the hole where the rattlers were hanging out. The danger must be really close to me now. And as my head was slowly turning there, I could see that the viper stretched to the max, apparently trying to get onto my shoulder. Now I still haven't found the dangerous part, the head.

I lowered my body toward the floor to prevent it from getting onto my shoulder, and then I saw the head with a forked tongue being licked at my face. I knew then that it had the opportunity to bite me in the neck but couldn't because of the LORD's Divine protection. Right then, I remembered what I said about the not bothering statement. So, I went over to the wood pile, picked out a 1" X 6" board, and proceeded to get a position to chop its head off because I still have a lot of students in here and do not want them to panic and injure one another if this reptile gets to the floor.

I placed the board against the wall planning to use it as a scissor when the snake backed up into the hole catching it about 4 or 5 inches behind the head with a quick shot across the hole with force.

Much to my surprise, this viper, while remaining stretched to the max, swung its whole body around toward the window and used its tail tip where the rattlers were to throw itself out of the hole and through the air toward the window as in flight. It is said that serpents are wise. This one must have been to a degree in figuring out gravity because it is now floating through the air as in flying toward the window, and much above the window's height. I saw this in the way that it made the flight trajectory above the angle needed to get to the window, but at the arrival, point gravity had pulled it to a point below the window where I pinned and eliminated it against the brick wall about halfway between the bottom of the window and the floor.

To be accurate with this task, I had to follow the "flying" viper with the board almost against its body all the way from near takeoff to the destination point. I praise the LORD and SAVIOR JESUS for his Divine protection and accuracy. I had no idea a reptile could throw itself that far through the air using only a snap of its tail.

The next interesting event occurred when I was selected to be the First Sergeant of a Service Battery in the same post. I checked in there and held formations with the Commanding officer. I soon had to take the commanding officer's place myself as he wasn't there anymore. Still not an Officer but taking his place. After a short period of time I was selected to attend the Sergeants Major Academy at Fort Bliss, Texas. We had a lot of people attending there with preparation for placement in a Sergeant Major position in a unit somewhere more likely overseas.

After graduation, I received orders for assignment to Germany. I was very happy that I could take my wife with me now. We proceeded to the assigned location and were escorted by a member of the organization to get our quarters set up. All went very well for almost a year there. One day, on a field trip, we were up very early in the morning to load our equipment onto the vehicles and started on the road in convoy driving all day.

Late that afternoon, before dark, the soldiers were permitted to set up their bedding to rest. As fate would have it, the commanding officer remembered some items that were necessary for successful task accomplishment, so he selected the Sergeant Major to take a vehicle and return to the garrison to retrieve them. We were very tired, having been on the road all day and setting up operations. The Sergeant Major asked me to ride back with him to lend a helping hand.

I was watching over the men inflating their air mattresses by mouth when I found out that it would be a while before we could leave on the trip. So, I decided to sit down and lean back against this tree I was standing by to rest for a few minutes, knowing that the trip would take all night to go and return to the field. I cleared the leaves on the ground, hoping there were no sharp burrs there and the area looked good, so I slowly turned and started to sit as I was very tired.

The man closest to me was inflating his air mattress and looking toward the ground where I was headed to sit. Suddenly, I saw him throw himself through the air at great speed, as in a football tackle toward me, hitting me so hard that I landed about 15 or 20 feet from where I was standing. I yelled at him, asking why he did that. As I had no padding on to help absorb some of that shock. He said nothing but turned and pointed to the exact spot where I had almost sat down. A poisonous viper was coiled to strike me had I gone any lower. I wondered how it got there without me seeing it.

The only logical reasoning was that it was on the way to the sleeping bags while I was clearing a place to sit, and by the time I was to sit, it had arrived at that very same location. Again, I Praise and thank the LORD and SAVIOR JESUS for his Divine protection.

You perhaps are wondering why I spent so much time discussing poisonous vipers. It seems to me it was a practice by the enemy from my childhood on the earth until even now to try to steal, kill, and destroy me. Remember, it was the serpent used by the enemy that got to Adam and Eve in the garden of Eden. "And he said unto the woman, Yea hath God said, Ye shall not eat of every tree of the garden?" Genesis 3:1-5. So, why not use the same tactic against me with the subtle serpent, who has spent a lot of time in the woods and field where the vipers have existed from the time that I was a child until now? I feel that this is a very important subject matter to present.

My next move after that field trip was to make my retirement decision. I had already started planning to retire before the trip to Germany. It was a difficult thing to do because I would have to cut my tour short this time. Anyway, I made the final decision and retired. My wife and I left Germany and arrived on the United States East Coast. From there, we proceeded to Niagara Falls on the Canadian side just to look at it for a couple of hours, then headed to Michigan to visit some of her family there, then to Canada to visit more of them. Our next move was to head to Des Moines, Iowa, to visit her last family members.

Finally, with all of the family visits accomplished, we headed on the road with California as our planned destination. However, by the time we arrived in Colorado Springs, Colorado, I became very Ill with a stomach problem, so we decided to stay there for a few days for recovery. While there and feeling better, we decided to do some "sightseeing," as it is called, and in so doing, we saw a house for rent. Having enjoyed the sights there, we called to ask to rent that house, and it was available.

We rented it immediately and remained there for some time. I even got a job to help decide if we should remain there for an unspecified time. Our family from Iowa visited us regularly, so we decided against going to California.

After being there for a few weeks, I started working with an Employment Agency and getting job offers from the US Post Office. I accepted the Mail Carrier job then the Government Civil Service sent me a request for a job interview in Denver, Colorado. I was accepted, and we moved to Denver. One day, while working that job, I got four more offers. After checking each of them with an interview, I went to work with the one at the US Fish and Wildlife Service. We moved the office to a different location and found it was the same distance from home as the previous location.

One evening, on my way home, while riding my bicycle, I was struck by a car. There was so much that happened I will hold it for another time and place. While I was recovering at home, lying there in bed, I saw a majestic vision. There was a huge stage setting with beautiful drapes with "tiebacks" where I could see the opening between them. Then, a platform came out from the right side, floating on nothing but air (or the word of GOD), having a Lamb as white as snow lying on it looking straight at me, then stopped at the perfect center of that stage. I asked the LORD what that meant. He said, "I have given you a Lamb without spot or blemish to take away your sins." Next, I asked, "what is that platform He is riding on," then He said, "That is the Lambs Book of Life, and your name is written therein." This Lamb here 1s JESUS, our LORD and SAVIOR.

You see that Lamb without spot or blemish is our LORD and SAVIOR JESUS. I had been wondering why so much disaster was happening to me. This was the assurance I needed to rest in believing that I was and am on the right path of righteousness, not of myself, but with JESUS.

Please remember that you do not have to wait until you are the perfect person to receive JESUS. I, who have written this testimony, was a very bad person in my actions in connection with the world, so don't wait to think you have to be a good person to receive Jesus.

"Remember there was one who came and said unto JESUS, "Good Master, what good thing shall I do, that I may have eternal life?" And he said unto him, why callest though me good? There is none good but one, that is, God: but if thou wilt enter into life, keep the commandments."

(Matthew 19:16, 17)

Now that you have been well versed on what a great and Holy LORD and SAVIOR CHRIST JESUS is, you must be ready to take the next step and receive him into your heart.

"Therefore, being justified by faith, we have peace with God through our Lord Jesus Christ."

(Romans 5:1)

"Speaking of the word now: But what saith it? The word is nigh thee, even in thy mouth, and in thy heart: that is, the word of faith, which we preach; That if thou shalt confess with thy mouth the Lord Jesus, and shalt believe in thine heart that God hath raised him from the dead, thou shalt be saved. For with the heart man believeth unto righteousness: and with the mouth confession is made unto salvation."

(Romans 10: 8, 9 and 10)

Now for the invitation, Say, "Dear LORD and SAVIOR JESUS, I am a sinner and cannot save myself I want to be saved and born again by you, so I am asking you to forgive my sins and come into my heart and make me a new creation in you.

Thank you for saving me and giving me a place in the kingdom of Heaven Eternally with you."

All the foregoing scriptures were taken from the King James Version of the Holy Bible.

There are many more instances that I could mention with this writing, but I am getting the unction to hold those for perhaps another time and for them to be voiced rather than written. After all, I am not trying to write a library but tell you about JESUS.

In doing all of this writing, I do hope that I have explained enough to prove to you the most important reason why you need JESUS.

As Jesus said, "I am the way, the truth, and the life; no man cometh unto the Father but by me."

That one reason is enough for me.

www.ingramcontent.com/pod-product-compliance
Lightning Source LLC
Chambersburg PA
CBHW051245120626
46547CB00014B/1801